MARYLEBONE
versus
THE WORLD!!

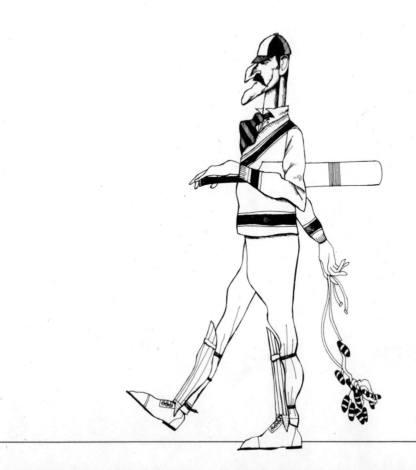

First published in Great Britain in 1987 by
Pavilion Books Limited
196 Shaftesbury Avenue, London WC2H 8JL
in association with Michael Joseph Limited
27 Wrights Lane, Kensington, London W8 5TZ

Text and illustrations © William Rushton 1987
Designed by Lawrence Edwards

British Cataloguing in Publication Data
Rushton, William
    Marylebone versus the world.
    I. Title
    828′.91409   PN6175

ISBN 1-85145-099-8

Printed and bound in Great Britain

Contents.

CONTINUED OVERLEAF

YOURS !

CONTENTS CONTINUED

Prologue.

'Hello, God!' said the Holy Ghost, gaily leaping through the French windows with his head and three tennis racquets under his arm, 'and what are You up to?'

'A bit of creating,' replied God. 'How about you?'

'Well, I think we've nearly got this Tennis thing together,' said the Holy Ghost, putting the racquets back in the Hairy Mammoth's foot Umbrella Stand.

'A wimpish game!' cried God. 'All right for girls. Bonk, bonk. To and fro with a soft ball. But *this* is the fellow, this is the game of the future.' He waved a round, red leather thing. 'This one's far too good to go through the monasteries. That's OK for Tennis and Golf and Beggar-your-Neighbour and Football – but this one I'm giving straight to the laity.'

'What's so good about it?' asked the Holy Ghost, somewhat peevishly.

'Well,' said God, 'it's longer for a start and has decent intervals for lunch and tea. I mean to say, you can't have tea and crumpets and cucumber sandwiches in the middle of a football match, can you? This is a long game, with a good, hard ball. Cop that!' And God threw the round, red leather thing to the Holy Ghost who caught it and squealed with pain. 'This is a creation!' A nasty fit of coughing obliged Him to stub out half a Passing Cloud on a passing cloud. 'Why on Earth,' He thought, 'did I create Tobacco? Must have had something in mind. A cure for cancer? Perhaps I meant cattle to eat it. Or was that marron glacés?'

The Holy Ghost was still sucking the pain out of his fingers. 'Dare I enquire to whom You will grant this game?'

'Someone pretty special,' boomed God. 'Hand me the A-to-Z. I shall open it at random and stick a pin in a page, as punters do to find winners in the Good Book.'

'*The Sporting Life?*'

'The Bible, you idiot.' And closing his bright blue eyes, God brought His Great Finger down on an open page.

'Mary-le-Bone,' pronounced God, quite slowly as He had forgotten his glasses (and also wasn't that certain how to pronounce it).

'Marylebone?' echoed the Holy Ghost. 'That's all Specialists in Rare Arabian Diseases.'

'Not yet,' said God, and began to idly wonder who Mary-le-Bone was. Surely, Mary-*la*-Bone for starters. Anyway, with this new game about to burgeon in the borough, beatification seemed only right: *Saint* Mary-le-or-la-Bone. He was sure she deserved it.

'If I was You,' said the Holy Ghost, 'I'd get it under way in the *North* of England. They'll do it properly. You'd never have got whippet-racing or pigeon-fancying off the ground in Mary-le-Bone.'

'No. No,' said God. 'London needs the grassy bits. I assure you, the grounds are a good size. And very pretty. The grass will be mown in stripes. There will be marquees and great pavilions. The players will be dressed all in white, and the games will last for days and days, at the end of which, on many occasions, there will be no result whatsoever.'

The Holy Ghost roared with laughter. 'You're joking, aren't You?'

'I have never been more serious,' replied God, and this was true. Most of the business of Creation had been effected with tongue firmly set in cheek.

'What are You going to call this game?' asked the Holy Ghost, still inwardly tittering.

And at that moment – not by chance, of course, for is it not all meant to be? – there was a vigorous chirping from the long grass outside the French windows, as one of God's creatures got his legs over.

'Grass-hopper,' smiled God, 'it shall be called Grass-hopper, and We shall call the place where it is played – God's.'

And verily, verily, yea, and a few more verily's, in the foulness of time, thus came it to pass, or bloody nearly.

Introduction

Dear Lewis,

You have written to me most cordially asking if I would, as the Marylebone Cricket Club's oldest living member, write an Introduction to your book. Let me say at once that I shall be honoured so to do. This is, when all is said and done, the *Official* History of that Great Institution, and not the pirate work that some worthless young toad-shagger called Ashton or Rushbag is working on. He has approached many of the older members, including myself, imploring us in a most obsequious note to 'blab' on the Club, and to 'give him the dirt' on many events, both past and present. Suffice it to say that he has offered pitifully small sums of money, and as if bribery was not enough, which it isn't, has even stooped, in the case of the murder of Umpire Bird, to blackmail. Our lips, I assure you, Mr Lewis, are sealed. Only to you will the murky secrets of the Bodyline tour be revealed. You alone will learn what happened to C. P. 'Choker' Renshaw's pickled head.

I have been a member of the MCC now for two hundred years, well over a hundred of those as a *playing* member, so not much has gone on without my knowing all about it. The ill-fated tour of Papua New Guinea, for instance. I was there. No, I wasn't.

My fellow-members and I are both ready and willing to be pumped and probed. We are determined that *your* book, Mr Lewis, shall tell the whole truth and nothing but the truth, and that Mr Rushbag's book shall be revealed for what it undoubtedly will be – a scurrilous cat-bag of mendacity and misrepresentation. He shall be branded as a Truth-Economist.

We have reached that age when the appearance of men in white jackets no longer means that the Umpires are coming out. Best now that the Truth be known.

Yours,

Thomas Lord.

Thomas Lord was a Yorkshireman, and thus being born a mercenary bastard with an eye ever open for the main chance, at the first opportunity he drifted south, set himself up in the wine trade and became to all intents and purposes the Professional to the White Conduit Club, a rather classy cricket club in Islington.

There were at that time (1785-ish) large sums of money to be made from cricket. The Aristocracy were constantly betting vast amounts on single-wicket encounters between themselves or their Champions, therefore there were fortunes to be made in side-bets, rake-offs, back-handers, the rigging of matches, the 'nobbling' of players. It was also in those days an extremely cheap game to organise. There were no team sweaters or flannels; gentlemen simply removed their coats. There were no pads or gloves or abdominal protectors; a bat was a single lump of spliceless rough-hewn teak. The New Ball was taken approximately every three years.

So when two of the most distinguished Patrons of the Game, the Earl of Winchilsea and the Duke of Richmond (whose wife was later to run the extremely successful pre-Waterloo Ball), asked Lord to set up a new ground for the White Conduiters, at their expense, Tom Lord was in like Flint. He rented a field to the north of the Marylebone Road. Not much was happening in those parts, it was almost entirely rural. To the south, in what would one day be Harley Street, various barbers and carpenters were setting up establishments, having realised that their talents with the razor, the pliers and the saw could be put to much greater financial advantage in the medical profession. Adjacent ponds were ideal for the breeding of leeches.

The first Lord's was in what is now Dorset Square, and the White Conduit Club moved there in 1787. In 1788, the White

Conduit Club became the Marylebone Cricket Club. This was (a) very lucky for Colin Cowdrey, who would otherwise have been W.C. Cowdrey, and (b) means that the MCC were only 199 years old at their Bicentenary.

The Duchess of Richmond's Ball.

THE
M.C.C.
CAT

peter

LORD
WINCHILSEA

AN
UNFORTUNATE
FOWL

Thomas Lord's First Ground.

In the late eighteenth century, as today, no open, green space in London was safe from the avaricious clutches of Property Speculators and Estate Agents. Thomas Lord was therefore not here long, but the interest in this rare study of the ground is not in the cricket match portrayed but in the two figures on the bench. For many years it has been taken for granted that these were the first gentlemen to keep the score on paper, as opposed to the traditional method of carving notches or 'scoring' on a piece of wood. In fact, it is now revealed, the two gentry are no less than William 'Hindblind' Hickey, so-called for his extraordinary lack of wisdom even after the event, and Neville Distemper, his fellow-diarist. This odious pair of Grub Street hacks were ever on the QV for salacious gobbets about cricketers that they would pass

Happily for cricket the dawn of the nineteenth century witnessed the births of Jolly Jack Woodcock (*above*) and E. W. Swanton (*overleaf*).

on, suitably embroidered, to any unsavoury journal that would pay them sufficient for porter and tobacco. They expressed no interest in the game whatsoever, but sought out only malicious gossip and rumour. Not for them the stirring activities of such as Ned 'Lunger' Binns as he smote the White Heather Club to every part of the ground, but one mild indiscretion by the Lunger behind the Pavilion and all London was to hear of it. Even Lord Winchilsea was not safe. Yet again it was not his bowling that attracted their unsavoury gaze, his magnificent grubbers that decimated the ranks of Highgate, but were his Lordship's pudgy fingers to dally even momentarily within the bodice of a serving-wench at tea, then all eyes were upon him.

Ye Anciount Scorer.

Blame me, I don't know, I don't understand these blasted Bonus Points - Decimal Points for scoring 2.7 runs in 3.5 overs in 1.09362 days (less Average Rainfall - 4.32701 ins) plus Average Crowd of 8.23274 per diem, less Poundage of Bats, Less Length of Grass, Weight of Umpires, Size of Balls, etc., etc., It's the end of Notching as We Know It.

AN EXTRAORDINARY GAME.

An extraordinary Game of Cricket played at LORD'S, between two teams of WOMEN! On one side a most gracious XI – Lady Wives of Marylebone members. On the other Lady Friends of Mr. Thomas Rowlandson, a motley gang of fleshy Tarts. 'Never again' vouchsafed the Members, 'NEVER'.

Lord's Second Ground.

In 1811, Thomas Lord, anticipating an alarming rise in the rental and subsequent bum's rush, upped his turves and moved his ground northwards towards St John's Wood. Once again, the MCC were not to be there long; this time Parliament elected to drive the Regent's Canal straight through it.

There was time, however, for this Match to be played, the first of only two occasions that ladies have been allowed to play on the MCC's hallowed acres. The second occasion was in 1976 when the English ladies played Australia, an exercise the MCC has not cared to repeat for what, according to Sir Rambo, is a very good reason.

'Danger to members, old chap. I was there. England were batting, and dear old "Bushy" Trencher-Foote was sitting next to me in the Long Room, only mildly the worse for gin. I noticed that he'd made a low, groaning sound when the English openers passed near us, but I'd put this down to wind, to which "Bushy" has ever been a martyr. However, when the first wicket fell and England's Number Three strode past us, I followed his gaze, and hearing again the same low groan, realised that "Bushy", like many of us, had never previously seen an England cricketer's thighs, and damned fine thighs they are too. Fine, smooth, brown muscular thighs, deliciously set off by the short white skirt and well-blancoed pads. Well, to cut a long story short, while I was able to contain myself, mainly by thinking of Geoffrey Boycott, it was to prove all too much for "Bushy". The fifth wicket fell, and through the Long Room came her successor, a strapping blonde all-rounder with thighs the colour of caramel. With a single bound, and an agility unexpected in a man whose bus pass is personally signed by King Edward VII, he was within a yard of the bonny creature. He had his back to me, but I immediately conjectured from his vigorous movement and her running screaming to the wicket, that he had, in the parlance of the Gutter

Press, exposed himself. Of course, the whole bloody business was hushed up. "Bushy" was put down, and the gel's behaviour was written off as Pre-Menstrual Tension. And that was that re Women's Cricket at Lord's. And quite right too. Poor old "Bushy".'

The Present Ground.

For the last time Thomas Lord moved his turves and deposited them on the ground we know today. At an angle. He then began to think about selling a good part of the ground to Property Developers. He put it round that if any honest entrepreneur was thinking of building a few squares and crescents, hotels perhaps, or sought to enlarge the canal, or push a railway-line north, was thinking in terms, perhaps, of a station, then St John's Wood was a likely spot and Tom Lord had a slice of it. Thus did the devious Yorkshireman apply the squeeze to the membership, who were not surprisingly extremely upset. The day was saved by the MP for the City of London, William Ward, who was also a director of the Bank of England and therefore never troubled by the thought of whence his next luncheon interval was coming. £5,000 he paid out, a considerable sum in those days, and if there was any justice (which there isn't but that's another tome entirely) the ground would be known as Ward's. Chances are it would be if Tom Lord's name had been Entwhistle or Owlthwaite.

Incidentally, as a ground it was a disgrace. The outfield was maintained by a flock of sheep, and as to the pitch itself most counties refused to play on it. It may however have inspired Alfred Mynn to evolve round-arm bowling in the search for greater pace. On one occasion he managed to make one lift so viciously that it carried the batsman's top hat as far as long stop, who caught it.

Mister
Thomas Lord
Meets Ye
Estate
Agent
in a
Field
in St.
John's Wood.

Pay ye no heed, Sire, to any ill-considered, nay, pig-ignorant prattle on the subject of a Slope.

Likewise, Sire, pooh-pooh any ridiculous rumours you may be privy to about a hump or ridge.

The Bribing of the Umpires.

The Murder of Umpire Bird.

That picture opposite, The Bribing of the Umpires (and it still goes on today, mark my words, no names, no mandrills), reminds me, Mr Lewis, that I was going to reveal all about the murder of Umpire Bird. A case that would have baffled Agatha Christie, who wouldn't have been allowed in the Pavilion anyway. It happened during that Centennial Test and, of course, could not be allowed to mar the occasion. Not that the weather helped. Anyway, that's what caused the commotion between a couple of members and Umpire Bird, and the intervention by the police. This is all well-documented and in the public domain and damned bad form in my view. Not so well-known, in fact, well buried under the red and yellow carpet that graces the Committee Room is what happened next. Umpire Bird, supported by two constables, entered the Long Room and as he passed me I took the opportunity of expressing the general view: 'Silly Bugger!' He turned as if to riposte and fell into my arms. There was a Swiss Army knife sticking out from between his shoulder blades. The reflexes are still pretty quick for a man of my enormous age, and I swiftly hung my hat on it.

'Poor chap's fainted,' I cried, 'Don't worry, I am a qualified midwife.' And gesturing to my friend 'Bonker' Tosspot (Kent and Prussia) I took Bird's legs, Bonker his ears, and we carried him briskly downstairs to the Gentlemen's Lavatory. We locked ourselves in a vacant stall. 'Summon the Committee,' I cried to Jagger, the lavatory's custodian, and in no time a quorum had been formed, albeit somewhat cramped, and an Extraordinary General Meeting called.

There was immediately a unanimous vote for a cover-up. I then proposed that the only hope was to find a *doppelgänger* for the late Bird, which ironically was already beginning to gather worms.

'Through the Chair, what is a *doppelgänger*?'

'A double, a dead-ringer, a twin.'

'With respect, not an easy task, and he's inspecting the wicket in five minutes.'

'We need a man who looks like a weasel.'

'More, through the Chair, like a hatchet.'

'A tortoise in my view.'

'He's a swarthy fellow, or was.'

'I do feel, Mr Chairman, that it is stretching the boundaries of good taste somewhat to stand on the body of a loyal servant of the club and compare him to tortoises and swarthy weasels.'

'Point taken, but does anyone know of such a person in the Marylebone area on whom we can lay hands in the next five minutes?'

(Total silence)

'Begging your pardons, gentlemen, but I do,' cried Jagger from beyond the door. After some technical wrangling, he was elected to the Committee, in time to propose and fetch a Lebanese laundryman from the Edgware Road.

This obviously explains some of Umpire Bird's rather bizarre decisions of late, but our friend is learning all the time. His lips are sealed on a monthly basis, and so far no-one has seen through his disguise.

They will now, of course, once this book of yours is out, Mr Lewis, but I made you a promise and anyway will it not cheer a rainy summer's day to hear cricket lovers abusing 'Umpire Bird' in whatever lingo they speak in Lebanese launderettes?

The Second Pavilion.

Emerging from the second pavilion erected on Lord's ground in 1874 is one of the most extraordinary cricket teams ever assembled. It is thought to be a humorous retort by one O. P. Rogers-Boyes, an intimate of Oscar Wilde and something of an 'aesthete', who had not been selected for the Marylebone team for three seasons. The reason, he suspected, was that he was not a Freemason. It is more likely that his rich variety of Toilet Waters and Unguents upset his fellows in the changing room. However, this team was his revenge. Here it is in batting-order:

1. C. V. P. Brown-Hatter
2. N. J. Shirtlifter
3. Buggery A.
4. S. D. P. Turd-Burglar
5. O. P. Rogers-Boyes (capt.)
6. Bender L.
7. Crouch P.
8. H. O. Roaring-Poofter
9. Fairy G.
10. Bent V.

and bringing up the rear an Indian doctor from the Docklands –

11. R. V. Bumbandit

Tradition has it that the MCC lost rather badly, but all records of the game have disappeared.

The Pavilion As We Know It.

A contest was held amongst architects for the design of the New Pavilion. It was won by one Montgomery Carbuncle with a design that had only recently been rejected for the Grand Hotel, Brighton. The Committee had been looking for 'shabby grandeur'. Carbuncle's proud boast was that it could sit the entire membership – admittedly only in acute discomfort. There had been a number of specifications such as an enormous cellar, to house not only sufficient alcoholic refreshments for the members, but also a working Morgue. At any one moment, it could contain at least twelve dead members. (One of the reasons for the extreme age of the MCC member is that, so long is the waiting list that many are not elected until well into their nineties.) Another specification was that the accommodation for the professionals should be a decent distance from the amateurs' dressing-rooms, and down-wind.

A Brilliant Scheme.

To prevent any unpleasantness in the Pavilion when the Sight-Screens are shifted.

1. As the Sight Screen moves South, by an intricate system of wires & pulleys a body of members, is moved North.

2. The Members arrive at the next window, fresh and fit. Well played!

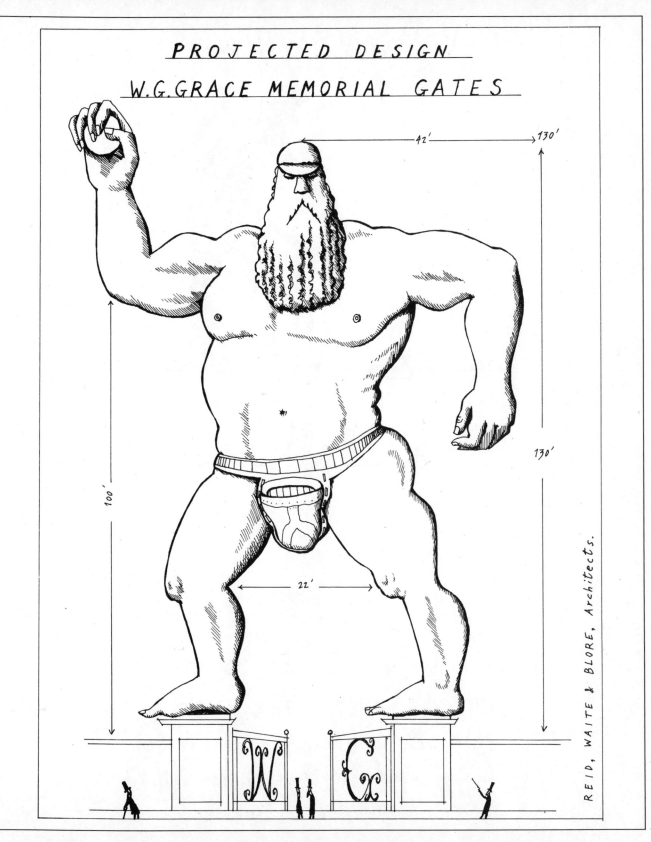

PROJECTED DESIGN
W.G. GRACE MEMORIAL GATES

REID, WAITE & BLORE, Architects.

A Major Mystery.

WHY do the MCC have a weather-vane with a likeness of the famous baggy-nosed Scots comedian Billy Connolly thereon?

Minutes of the MCC Buildings & Works Committee.

'You are proposing a motion about the Tavern.'

'Thank you, Mr Chairman. I don't know, Gentlemen, if any of you have been to the lavatory recently –'

'Through the Chair –' (Cries of 'Shame!', 'Filthy business!', 'Dirty Swine!')

'I refer, Mr Chairman, to the lavatory at the Nursery End – the *Gentlemen's* lavatory, I hasten to add – with the corollary that the term "Gentlemen" is used advisedly as a close inspection of that building will reveal that it is no more than a Poste Restante for every homosexualist – every pervert –'

'Are you suggesting, Sir, that homosexuals pursue the Noble Game?'

'I've known a few –'

'Name names!'

(A whispered response unheard by the Secretary.)

'But – NOT – Good Lord! We've shared a coat-hook!'

'He's rubbed my back with embrocation!'

'He has worn my boater!'

'Mr Chairman, if I may continue. Have you seen the lavatory walls? The graffiti? Filth and innuendo. I quote: "I shall be wearing a green carnation and carrying a copy of Wisden's Almanack. Meet me at the Grace Gates." Unquote. There are references to the length of umbrellas. To the size of hats. My God, horse-whipping is too – too –'

'Too damned expensive, I find, since Mavis died.'

'And where do the buggers congregate? Where do the pansies blossom and bloom?'

'Where? Where?'

'I'll tell you where. Outside the Tavern, that's where. With their long umbrellas and their sizeable hats. Cinema organists, hairdressers, interior decorators, television personalities, pornographers with leftist leanings and baggy-nosed comedians. What to do? you cry.'

'What to do? What do to?'

'My answer is a simple one, and tinged with the necessary brutality. Demolish the Tavern! As God, in his infinite disgust, rained gall-stones and coals of fire upon Sodom and Glocomorrah, let us wreak proper vengeance upon the posturing deviants!'

'Vengeance! Vengeance! Gall-stones! Coals of fire!'

'And while the team of honest demolitionists exact their toll upon the Tavern with their Great Ball and glorious picks, what about the Clock Tower?' (Cries of 'Too pretty by half!', 'A phallic symbol if ever I saw one!') 'What about the Clock Tower? Have I not also seen writ upon those lewd walls – "Meet me under the Clock Tower at tea-time, ducky. I am lithe and lovely."' (Cries of 'Burn! Burn! Destroy! Destroy! Loot! Ravage! High explosives are too good for them!')

CIGARETTE CARD Nº27

P. Q. STUTTER

JACK LUNATIC

R. HERPE

BOGG. N.J.

TARQUIN HAWKER

The Corinthians.

21 . P. F. ('Plum') Warner

SIR GERBIL STENCH

The Corinthians.

Dear Lewis,

You ask me about the Corinthians, the giants of my youth. The likes of C. B. Fry, who went to Lord's armed with 'Hock and Herodotus, lobsters and strawberries' – and thought Hitler had some remarkably sound ideas. Lord Hawker-Harrier, who ran Lord's with a rod of iron for over a hundred years, until he tried to split the atom with a mashie-niblick. He had the heavy roller run over a professional who had called him a bastard (very *sotto voce*) for cuffing him severely after he had been out for 99. Nevertheless, there was many an old pro who said it was a pleasure and a privilege to lick the Blanco off his pads. How he loved that!

Ah, memories! The trouble, you see, with this Great Nation Today is that it's not casting men in the heroic mould of yore. Vast men we used to have – great, snorting, red-necked Heroes who could only be decently clad by Soft Furnishings. Men who could lead an expedition against some recalcitrant Tibetans of a morning and still shoot 87 on the old Royal Lhasa Golf Course prior to Tiffin.

To my mind the greatest of them all was O. W. P. Bread, a hero so self-effacing that you may never have heard of him. If only he'd taken up that massive offer from MGM. A million dollars a year and first use of Tallulah Bankhead. His obituary from the *Daily Telegraph* lies before me as I write. I knew him quite well.

Out of General Gordon by Captain Oates – not, of course, the Captain Oates who staggered out of Captain Scott's Antarctic tent gallantly shouting into the teeth of a blizzard – 'There's never a bloody taxi when you want one!' Not he, but his mother, Captain Winnie Oates of the Women's Royal Horse Artillery.

I'll quote you some of the Obituary – it makes moving reading. 'O. W. P. Bread was a sporting loony of the Old School. A true Blue. Eton, Harrow, Winchester, Balliol, Wadham, Gomorrah, Christchurch. He played Cricket for England, Rugby for

Wales and Soccer for the Highest Bidder.

'He played in that great European Cup-winning side of 1908 – Vatican City. What a line-up: Cardinal in goal; Cardinal and Cardinal at full-back; Cardinal, Cardinal and Cardinal at half-back; and a forward line of Cardinal, Cardinal, Cardinal, Pope and Bread.

'O. W. P. Bread was then sold to Lady Violet Bonham-Carter for an undisclosed fee.

'For some years O. W. P. Bread held the World 400-yard Tango Record. You may remember the occasion when so vigorously did he compete, so profusely did he perspire, that the Union Jack so proudly emblazoned on his sporting trouser ran into a Purple Badge of Courage.

'He swam the Channel in full evening dress and then walked to Paris that he might have dried off in time for dinner at Maxim's. He turned down the Kingship of Bohemia on the grounds that it would have interfered with his winning of the Grand National on the stout, freckled back of Dame Nellie Melba.

'He was the epitome of the English Gentleman, who, but for a misguided attempt to vault up Everest – the pole snapped on the South Col and Fortnum's had packed a faulty hamper – would have been one hundred again on Wednesday.

'Still, he died as many of us would wish to have lived, shouting the Complete Works of Horace at a startled Sherpa.

'It was for this that the Queen, or the King as she then was, awarded him a posthumous.'

MCC versus the Public Schools.
by O.W.P. Bread.

Of all the cricket I played for the MCC, the games I most enjoyed were those against the Decent Schools. I would invariably skipper the MCC on such occasions, and the teams would be a subtle blend of experience and youthful exuberance, Amateur and Professional. It may seem odd to you in retrospect, but at the time, m'Lud, it seemed entirely natural to me, that I made a point of always changing with the boys in the Pavilion. To be surrounded by young, fit, hairless bodies in various forms of undress I have never failed to find wholly invigorating. I felt also that the boys gained strength from my presence. An old hand encouragingly squeezing a young thigh, the friendly pinch of a cheek – how does that thing of Sir Henry Newbolt's go? His captain's hand on his shoulder smote? Well, I think boys relish a little shoulder-smoting.

Let us be frank, there can be no stronger bond of comradeship betwixt men than to bathe together after strenuous exercise. There are those who will try to compare that feeling unfavourably with the love of a good dog or indeed a good wife, but not if they have savoured the camaraderie of the communal bath, the blur of pink, wet limbs through the steam, the shock of cool tile upon one's back, the brisk rubbing-down of each other's bodies with rough towels, that warm, tingling sensation spreading through one's groin, the –

(to be concluded)

From his personally-designed Eyrie on the roof of the Pavilion Sir Rambo Legge-Brake hurls advice at his batsmen.

RETIRE
HURT
AT ONCE,
YOU
USELESS
BASTARD!

he would cry.
And foolish
the batter
who did not
take the
next ball
between
the eyes.

Edwin Pratt-Buller & his Odious Dwarf Turnbull.

Edwin Pratt-Buller.

The story of Edwin Pratt-Buller is a tragic one. That he was a true Corinthian there is no doubt. There is no doubt either that you, gentle reader, have never heard of him. There is the tragedy. He would have played for England more often had he not refused to travel anywhere without his odious dwarf, Turnbull. This, despite his tremendous prowess with bat and ball, counted heavily against him when MCC teams were selected for tours of the Colonies. While the creature Turnbull's unsavoury antics could be tolerated at Lord's, where a member of the ground staff was appointed for the day to put Turnbull in a cricket-bag and sit on him, this was not a facility one could ask to be provided in, say, Melbourne or Calcutta. What was the extraordinary hold that the odious dwarf had over Pratt-Buller? Perhaps it is best not to know, but merely to shake one's head sadly and murmur, 'Tragic'.

The Ranjitsinhji Photograph.

" At last it can be revealed how I achieved this remarkable picture"

Lord Ben Nevis Photographer to the Rich.

Silver-Bollocks Bedlam.

The first Abdominal Protection of any sort was worn at Lord's in 1853. This is how the story goes. Joshua 'Silver-Bollocks' Bedlam was playing for the Gentlemen of Reigate against the Marylebone Club. As was his wont, prior to batting, usually at the fall of the fourth wicket, he was circumnavigating the ground, pausing at every tent or marquee for a little refreshment and badinage. He was always a popular figure wherever lovers of the Noble Game and Strong Drink were assembled, and never more so than in the tent belonging to the Irish Peers. He was downing a tankard of fizz when he became aware that no less a person than Oonah, Lady Clackspanker was probing his privates with the ferrule of her parasol.

'Odds Fish,' she exclaimed, 'but ain't ye the bulgy wonder?'

'Thank 'ee, M'Lady,' replied Bedlam, ever affable in drink.

'But are ye not afeared, Master Bedlam,' riposted Lady Clackspanker, ever the coquette, 'that that grand *sac d'oeufs* may be cracked asunder by yonder leathern ball?'

'Lawks, Ma'am, but I has King Willow 'twixt my manhood and the hurtling prune.'

'Nary enough!' she cried, 'for these are National Treasures! Ope up your breeks!'

Joshua Bedlam did so with a will, for even though they were in full view of a goodly audience, it was 1853 and everyone had had a few.

'Stuff these in as a buffer,' said M'Lady, thrusting twelve used napkins into the gaping vent.

'There's room for more,' laughed Silver-Bollocks uproariously. 'Your wicker hat, I fancy, will keep everything neatly stored,' and with a single movement he removed Lady Clackspanker's gay *chapeau* and rammed it down his trouser.

'Fie! Fie!' she giggled prettily, and though they had never met before, a bond was forged, and for the next forty years or more he gave her one every other Thursday afternoon, when collecting a fresh bonnet to protect his working parts.

Silver-Bollocks Bedlam.

The Appalling Effect of Pilcher's Hat-Knocker.

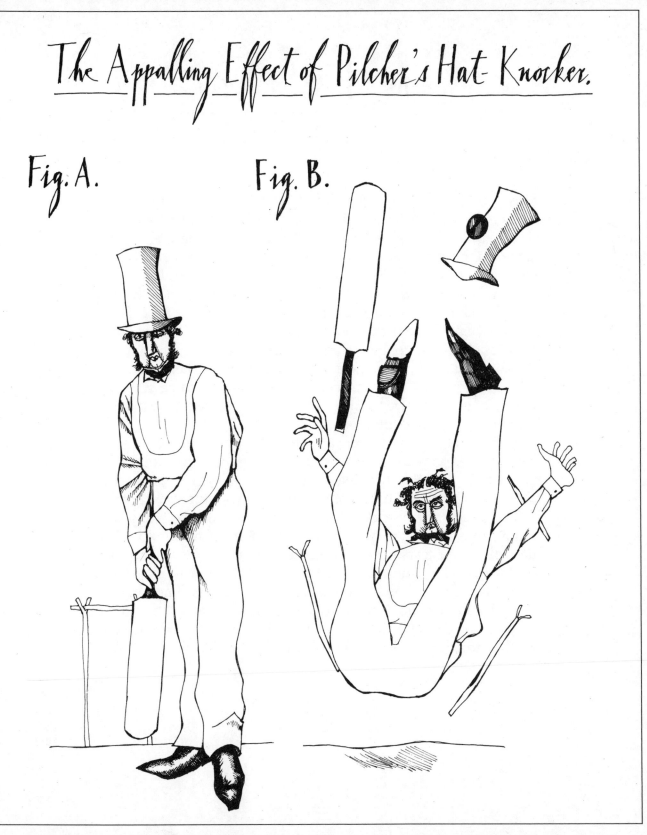

Fig. A.

Fig. B.

The Lobsters.

This is G. H. Simpson-Hayward of Worcestershire, known as the Last of the Great Lobsters. He took over four hundred wickets in his career. In the 1909 MCC tour of South Africa he was the most successful English bowler, taking twenty-three wickets in the Tests and fifty-nine overall. Now the question is, if the lob was capable of such feats how come nobody lobs any more? Oh, you'll hear the older members decry the passing of spin, the demise of the 'leggie', the tweaker, but even the most ancient never spare a thought for the passing of the lobbist. Perhaps the First German War is to blame, perhaps the disappearance of matting wickets, on which Simpson-Hayward was particularly successful; suffice it to say, they have gone for ever. And yet they knew halcyon days. This is Pettigrew, an early demon of the lob:

'Preparatory to delivering the ball, he would rise like a ballet-dancer on point, pirouette slowly, then paw the ground with his foot. He would then lean forward, and having pressed his forehead to Mother Earth, would rise sharply to attention, stiff as a Coldstreamer, then stride forward, clutching the ball under his armpit, thus hiding his grip. At the last moment he would release the ball with a fearsome crack of his fingers. The fizzing pillock would strike the ground and leap from it at three or four times the pace, this velocity gained from Pettigrew's vicious fingering, the happy result of years spent as a fish-strangler. Many's the time he drew blood, grinding the batter's fingers against the handle of his bat.' My word, he was a crowd-pleaser!

G. H. Simpson - Hayward.

THE COLONEL'S
NOTORIOUS GRUBBER

The Art of Under-arm.

Mr PRESLEY'S
INFAMOUS SHOOTER

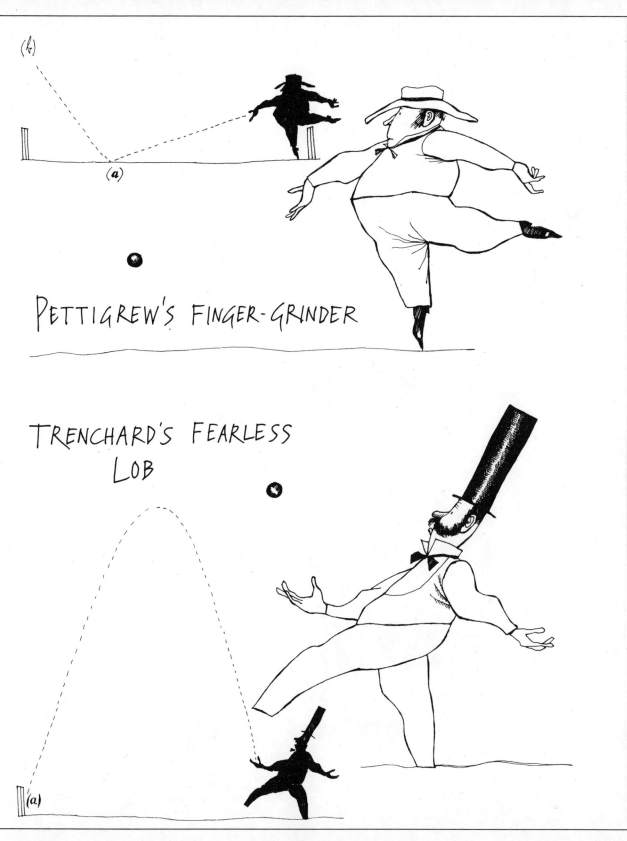

(b)

(a)

PETTIGREW'S FINGER-GRINDER

TRENCHARD'S FEARLESS
LOB

(a)

John Willes of Maidstone.

John Willes was the first to bowl overarm at Lord's. Not because he wore a hooped skirt, but more probably because he was a vicious bastard, driven mad by the one-way systems of his native heath, Maidstone. He was, quite rightly, no-balled, a decision that was upheld by an instantly-called committee who considered overarm bowling to be 'unfair'. John Willes immediately leapt upon his horse and rode away, never to be heard of again, unlike Andrew Lloyd Webber who picked up the ball at Soccer, and was responsible for the indescribably boring game of Rugby, and later for the equally tedious musical *The Half-Back of Notre Dame*.

The Quick Stuff.
The Len Yeoman Affair.

Arthur Stomach (Lancashire and England) kisses and tells:

'Aye! I remember it as if it were yesterday. The night before we had been invited to British Embassy in Calcutta for cocktails, and Len developed a powerful taste for Pink Ladies, which had previously been hard to come by in those parts. Truth to tell, he was still grossly drunk next morning and had to be supported to the wicket. He were given new ball, in the hopes that this responsibility might sober him up. He fell several times during his run-up – this was explained away later by Skipper as a "dicky tummy". He did seem to gain strength with every ball; the exercise – the freshish air, the falling-over, the getting-up – was clearly doing him some good.

'Then came the unpleasantness, when, quite obviously in some sort of temporary coma, he set off on his run-up in the wrong direction, towards the sight-screen, and unleashed a beamer into the crowd, taking a native water-bearer between the eyes.

'The riot that followed led eventually to the Independence of India, the Rise of Mahatma Gandhi, and the beatification of Sir Richard Attenborough. Oo, he were a right piss-artist, Len Yeoman.'

Len Yeoman (Yorkshire & England) Writes:

'Nay! Nay! 'Appen 'twas never thus, lad. I were suffering from a severe dose of Mantovani's Revenge and our baggage-master Fergie Benson 'ad given me half-a-bottle of his mixture. Strong drink never passed our lips in those days. We had Pride in those days. Put on England cap and you became tea-total, a non-smoker, and as celibate as a fully paid-up monk. Be selected for an MCC tour and you were an Ambassador for your Country. Except for Arthur Stomach, who was a right piss-artist.'

The Selection Committee.

Lewis, old chap!

There's never smoke without fire. Look at all that fuss about MI5 and whether or not Harold Wilson worked for the KGB. Now, those rather ill-advised comments young Botham made about the Selection Committee were, truth be told, absolutely spot on the knob. Yes, the Selection Committee is housed in an attic under the eaves of the Pavilion, and, yes, they do relish a gin or two. And sometimes they get it right, let's be fair. And quite often they get it wrong. More often than not. Has gin done more to bring English cricket into disrepute than marijuana? Discuss.

Rambo Legge-Brake.

THE SPORTING SPIRIT DOWN UNDER

Lion (to Kangaroo): Well played, young sir!

Kangaroo: Ah, piss off, yer Pommy Bastard, or I'll give yer another great boot in the goolies!

Lion: Thank you very much.

MCC versus The Argentine.

These are some of the lads who first toured the Argentine, except for the fellow-me-lad on the left who is a Groucho. Inadvertently, these chaps may have been responsible for troubles to come. Most of the opposition were railway engineers and roadmakers of British extraction, but there was the odd local, usually a polo-playing playboy, bags of Brilliantine and razor-sharp moustaches. Now after one particularly convivial pre-match lunch, one of these Argy-Bargies asked if our lads fancied a bit of a wager. Well, of course, your Marylebone boys are never slow to chance their arms, and cried out, 'Name your bet!'

'We'll play you,' said the Argentinian, 'for the Malvinas.'

'Right!' said our skipper, who had absolutely no idea what a Malvina was, but was not going to admit as much in front of a foreigner. He did cock an enquiring eyebrow at the team, who shook their heads as one. The Argentinians were looking strangely excited, so our skipper bearded one of the railway engineers.

'Malvinas,' said the railway engineer, 'I think they're some sort of Pampas prune – or dwarf mules – or handbags made from herring-skin.'

'That's all right.' Our skipper breathed a sigh of relief. He'd had a nasty suspicion that it might be something valuable. 'All right, lads!' he cried. 'You can tuck into the llama-juice!' And they did. And they lost.

It was a day young Galtieri never forgot.

Autographed picture of Australians in England, 1888.

F. R. Spofforth.

Here is an early example of underhand methods being employed by the MCC against Australia, as opposed to overarm methods which were employed later by D. R. Jardine. F. R. Spofforth was the man they feared then, so they had this caricature produced, which suggests as you can see that the Demon was not entirely as other men. If anything, the effect of it was quite the reverse of what the MCC had in mind. 'When,' as one MCC member put it, 'the projectile is whistling about your ears and teeth at a hundred miles an hour, it really doesn't matter if the protagonist is on the Sodom Borough Council or 87-year-old Mrs Serena Bradley of The Elms, Penge; the results are the same – Pain, Discomfiture and the Briefest Tenure of the Wicket.'

The L. P. Basin Affair.

One of the saddest results of this ruse was the L. P. Basin Affair. L. P. Basin has the single distinction of being the only MCC player to be shot by his captain for cowardice. I can only quote from the Captain's Official Report to Lord's.

'The firing-squad was the only just solution in that L. P. Basin did shamefully retreat towards square leg for no less than three consecutive deliveries from F. R. Spofforth. This, despite the fact that he is a professional and has even been on a cigarette-card.'

The Committee agreed whole-heartedly with the Captain's decision, a vote of thanks was passed, as was the hat.

The Hat.

W. G. Grace on Tour - A Revelation.

Dear Lewis,

      Upon my soul, here's a scoop for you. I thought I had this picture somewhere. I've no idea how I got it, but it's rare. It's the only time these three ever met, and yet they were all the same person. Bit of a riddle, eh? Well, who do they look like, I ask you? Yes, they are all W. G. Grace. Well, they are in Australia. The Australians were terribly keen that W. G. should tour out there, and it was the last thing he wanted to do, but the money was good. So these three were hired. The one on the left used to bat, the one in the middle bowled and fielded, and the rather more mature gentleman used to socialise, an area in which W. G. himself was notoriously weak. They, or rather he, was, or were, extremely popular. Whether or not this trick was only worked on Australia I don't know, but wouldn't it be fascinating if the four Graces carried on to the end of his career? I suppose one simply took pot luck in the surgery.

Bodyline.

Get bloody Bradman! That was the call from Head Office. And quite right. Unless we could prevent him from scoring a couple of hundreds every time he went to the wicket we were up Shit Creek, New South Wales, without a proverbial. Rumour had it he'd been raised by Aboriginals since birth, sustained on a diet of wichity grubs, snake and boiled platypus brains. He spoke no English until he was sixteen (to this day it's halting). His keen eye, they say, came from fending off with his *nulla-nulla* showers of hunting boomerangs thrown by his playmates. This would certainly sharpen up the reflexes. I saw those black fellas at Lord's when they came over in 1868. We were all invited out on the ground after the game to pelt one of their number with balls. Never touched him. So that's the sort of thing we were up against. Big question – how?

I think, if my memory serves me right, that it was Hawker-Harrier who came up with the answer. In fact it was his second answer. His first answer was simply to kill him. Apparently, during a spell as Viceroy of India, Hawker-Harrier had adopted some Thuggee and brought them home as pets. These chaps could break a man's neck with a handkerchief, which sounds a bloody good trick to me. To cut a longish story short, the general feeling was that this was Going Too Far. Indeed, although one hesitated to mention the word in Hawker-Harrier's presence it was Unsportsmanlike. But, and I think this is where the British Genius for Compromise is first-rate, it would be quite sportsmanlike, certainly sportsmanlike enough, if we simply *tried* to kill him, within the Laws of the Game. On the field Hawker-Harrier was still toying with the Handkerchief Notion. He maintained that a trained man could undoubtedly get Bradman from short leg, but a ballistics expert, an Artillery General whose name escapes me, rose and proposed, through the chair, that a cricket-ball being, in the proper hands, a lethal weapon, it should therefore be sufficient for our needs. That was when Hawker-Harrier came up with his second answer, which was to all intents and purposes the very scheme that Douglas Jardine employed so skilfully Down Under in the winter of 32/33.

Hawker-Harrier had vast estates in the Nottingham area, and employed a large number of miners to maintain his unique collection of man-traps. 'Those chaps,' it was his proud boast, 'can dig a man-trap twelve feet deep inside an hour.' They could also, he opined, given their great strength and the proper encouragement, be turned into the fastest bowlers the world had ever seen. He at once instigated a crash programme in the Nursery at Lord's, where, *en passant*, C. B. Fry used to spend happy hours with his train-set and Arthur Shrewsbury first cut his teeth on his Nanny. The programme was in the hands of 'Ripper' Slingshot, the old Yorkshire professional, who in his time had been as quick as anybody and would perhaps have been the quickest had not some of his time been served at the pleasure of His Majesty for a triple manslaughter in Barnsley. He would have hung had the judge not been on the Yorkshire Committee, a fellow-Freemason, and a man who viewed any decrease in the population of Barnsley as a Godsend.

After a week or two, Slingshot had reduced the numbers of strapping miners from two dozen to two. 'These lads,' he boomed, pointing proudly to one Larwood and one Voce, 'will bring a new prosperity to the undertakers of Sydney, Melbourne, Adelaide and Brisbane.' The Committee was given a demonstration of their speed and accuracy as the two demons wreaked havoc upon targets erected in the nets. It was noted immediately that balls bounced speedily at the head either (a) struck the head or (b) would lob gently into the short-leg region. Hawker-Harrier's plan seemed fool-proof. The battered targets were burned, and all present sworn to a vow of silence.

Thus, when the Task Force headed south in the autumn of 1932 it was with renewed confidence that Donald Bradman could be contained. And very possibly killed. It made one proud to be English.

The Japanese Connection.

What then are the MCC hiding? Something pretty big, you're thinking, Mr Lewis, and you are absolutely right. Suffice it to say that if it got about, even today, for many of the participants are still alive (I checked out two this morning as they slept in the Long Room, and when I prodded them, one grunted 'Floreat Etona!' and the other was quietly sick over his club tie), precisely what the MCC were up to at the highest level, exchanging telegrams for instance with the Emperor Hirohito, governments might well fall.

It has taken some years for the whole story to fall into place, not for nothing was the President's Office known as the Cloak and Dagger Room, but it might be that the moment is now ripe to reveal all. Fifty years is a long time, and I shall feel better for getting it all off my chest. Anyway, I'm far too old to concern myself with falling governments. The key to the whole beastly business is the Emperor Hirohito's ambitious policy for expansion in the East. One must understand that he not only had his slanty eyes fixed on China and Manchuria but also the great wastes of Australia. For reasons I could never understand, he coveted Darwin.

You remember I wrote of an Artillery General, a ballistics expert, who spoke up in Committee. The fellow I couldn't put a name to. He was to be seen around the Long Room all that summer. And then never seen again. Now as the norm, the last person one would have suspicions about would be a General, Royal Artillery. But this fellow was *too* English, y'know. He was bloody short, but always immaculately turned out, and if his tie wasn't the Gunners', it was OE or the old Red and Yellow. But while he explained away the colour of his skin as the natural result of a recent and severe bout of jaundice, is there, I ask you, a condition 'you can pick up in the Far East' which causes your eyes to go off at an angle? No, I think, and I realise that these are pretty severe accusations to level at a fellow-member, if such he ever was,

The Japanese Fleet off
Sydney Cricket Ground.

The Mysterious
"Artillery General."

HOWZA!

that he was an agent of Hirohito. Now, whether Hawker-Harrier and Co. knew that is another kettle of fish, but it might explain that photograph of the Japanese fleet off Sydney Cricket Ground. Just ask yourself, old cock, did the wily Oriental want Australia out of the Empire, so that they could occupy great lumps of it without outside interference? Would Australia not have left the Empire, had we succeeded in killing Bradman? These are deep and beastly waters, Watson, are they not?

Now what, you may well ask, would have made Johnny Nippon think of cricket as a weapon of diplomacy? Surely, you will say, they don't know their Pavilion End from their Nursery End. Aha! Not so. The MCC, in their wisdom, had attempted to introduce cricket to Japan only a year previously during a British Trade Week in Tokyo. The Prince of Wales was there, and a vast number of Captains of Industry with bags of ideas for the Nips to pinch, and Hawker-Harrier and an MCC party.

The Japanese did not take to cricket at all. Their sporting

tastes tend towards the violent. They are always hitting each with something – great sticks and swords, and balls on chains, or their feet and hands, or, in the case of the more enormous Jappo, their massive bellies. They couldn't see cricket providing the sort of spectacle that sets the sporting crowds of Tokyo on the roar. They quite enjoyed the business of appealing, which they turned into a fearsome ceremony, the whole team leaping in the air as a man, and screaming 'How's That?' in a manner that would reduce the bravest umpire to a sweaty pool. However, the facts had to be faced, that a lively beamer delivered into the heart of a Japanese face makes very little difference, and the pleasure to a bowler of delivering a good blow into the batsman's groiny regions, is somewhat diffused by the fact that many Japanese are blessed with the ability to retract their testicles.

One damned funny thing – one of our hosts – an exponent of Baritsu – asked our wicket-keeper 'Knobby' Hume if he would not like to be a Master of Unarmed Combat. 'Knobby', apart from being blind as a bat due to his pioneering work up the Amazon of Self-Abuse, is also deaf as a post, and enquired of our host why he should wish to be the Master of a One-Armed Wombat. Damned funny thing.

Now, while the tour as such was a pathetic failure, the Powers That Be in Japan obviously saw in cricket a weapon that could be successfully turned against the British Empire.

♪ IF YOU WANT TO KNOW WHO WE ARE,
WE ARE XXII GENTLEMEN OF JAPAN!

Bodyline attack on the secret papers at Lord's

Bodyline bouncer at MCC

by Staff Reporter

OWNERSHIP of secret documents held at Lord's cricket ground by MCC about the Bodyline Test series against Australia is to be challenged by Cabinet Minister Lord Gowrie and his brother, Malise.

The papers originated with their grandfather, the first Earl of Gowrie, and they are the heirs of his estate.

At Lord's, the documents — the existence of which is not widely known — are referred to as 'the Gowrie papers.' It is thought they could shed new light on a sporting row which assumed international political dimensions and was the subject of a controversial TV series.

The papers were sent to MCC from Australia in the 1970s. Bona fide researchers have been told that they are not for inspection. Investigations last week, however, point to the conclusion that MCC has no legal right to these papers.

A third person to ask for a look is this reporter. Mr Bailey, a well-respected and well-liked man, wrote back in friendly fashion to say that 'unfortunately' he was 'bound by a Committee decision that the papers as such — and in their entirety — should not be made available.' He went on : 'This is largely due to the wish to preserve beyond peradventure the feelings of those living folk who could be seen as being mentioned in a less than complimentary light.'

If you think I'm romancing, Tony boyo, thumb through these cuttings and tell me there's not skullduggery afoot. Secrets, you see, and covers-up, missing documents, Earls and heirs. I promised you something pretty big, didn't I? Who are these 'living folk' whose feelings Mr Bailey is so keen to preserve beyond peradventure? Mr Bailey is, of course, or was (and I've got my own theories on that one) MCC Secretary, and as such would have a pretty keen nostril as to which folk are living and which dead. I believe it is the main qualification sought for in an MCC Secretary.

Who are they protecting? Funnily enough, that's the very question I put to old 'Plunger' Runcorn, whose last words were 'I'll tell you – Aaaaaaarrrgh!' as he slid off his bar-stool. Foul play, one imagines, but it's damned hard to tell at his age. If you can separate the arsenic from the alcohol in a system as clapped-out as Plunger's then you're a better man than the local Coroner. Still, I promised I'd tell you. *Not* D. R. Jardine, though he was a glutton for glory, and mad as a March Hatter. Same cap though, the one that drove the Hill barmy. Yes, a fellow-Harlequin. I rather fancy if Burgess and Maclean and Philby and Blunt had been at Oxford they'd have been Harlequins. Who was passionately opposed to the use of Bodyline prior to the tour, and wrote so in his newspaper and magazine articles? Who managed the tour? Who never said a word about it in Australia? Who could have stopped Jardine with a single word? Who, now you come to think of it, even looks a bit Nippo in retrospect?

Quite right. Plum. The Grand Old Man of the MCC. Not 'living folk' by a long chalk, but that's Bailey covering up. Expect his resignation soon. Plum's your man. Enough said.

August 1986

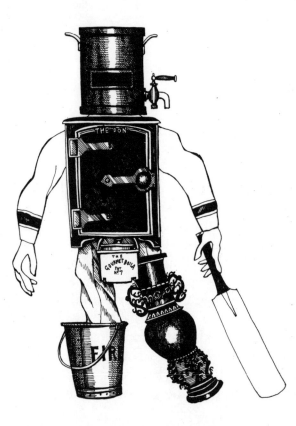

A. C. MacLaren, the only MCC tourist to learn anything from the Japanese about cricket. With this stroke he could carve a beamer in half, quite often scoring eight, that is a boundary past third man, and past long leg.

Absolutely Extraordinary Meeting of the MCC Committee & Mr Kevin Pecker, the Australian Entrepreneur.

'Well, Gentlemen, today is the day we put Mr Kevin Pecker to the sword, and send him back to Botany Bay with his tail between his legs.' ('Bravo! Hurrah! Well said!') 'To date one imagines that he sees himself very much as king of the castle, but he has not yet faced the full majesty of the MCC Committee. I think that by the end of this morning's session Mr Kevin Pecker will be grovelling at our feet, kissing the turn-ups of our trousers.' ('First rate! Whoopee! Yaroo!')

'Through the Chair, damned good idea to have the fellow in prior to luncheon. I know my Australian, and he's a different kettle of fish after lunch. As I know to my cost, that is no time to visit an Australian dentist.'

'When, Mr Chairman, is he due?'

'He should be cooling his heels in the Long Room now. I thought it a good idea to make him wait. Work up a bit of a muck-sweat. Perhaps finding himself in those august surroundings, that positively heave with Cricket's History, and not at his Woolloomoolloo whelk-stall or whatever, may make him see the error of his ways.'

'Through the Chair, there is a huge man standing at the door, in an ill-fitting double-breasted suit and a wide-brimmed hat with champagne-corks dangling from it.'

K. Pecker (for it is he): 'G' day, Gents! Pardon the intrusion, but I can't hang around all day waiting for you old farts to get your act together.' ('I say! Bloody rude! Upstart!') 'That Long Room of

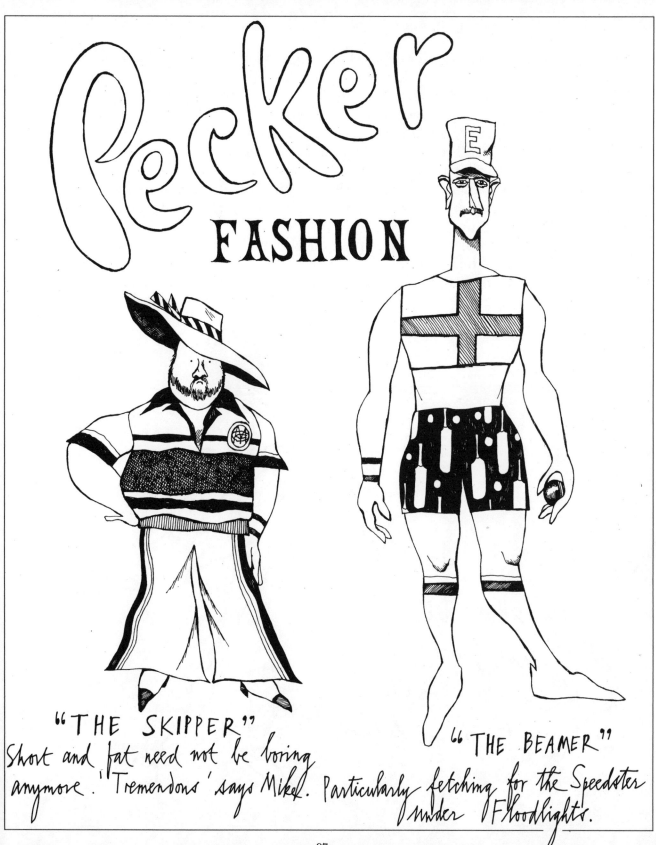

Pecker
FASHION

"THE SKIPPER"
Short and fat need not be boring anymore. 'Tremendous' says Mike.

"THE BEAMER"
Particularly fetching for the Speedster under Floodlights.

yours is about as exciting as skinny-dipping with Mother Theresa. Why don't you get One-Armed Bandits in? And some music so the old buggers can boogy a bit?'

'Mr Pecker! I must call you to order –'

'Don't try sticking your electronic roo-prodder up my arse, mate. Look, I've got you by the last remains of your wizened scrotes so all you've got to do is just listen up and I'll give you the shape of cricket to be, whether you like it or not. Right, synchronise your gold watches. As of now, it's the twentieth bloody century.'

'Matron, would you remove Sir Norbert? I think he's suffering from something terminal.'

'It'll be a beauty, Gents, a bottler! We'll play at night. There'll be no more boring old white bloody flannels. The teams'll be

"THE SHORT LEG"
Feel at ease, yet secure,
in the close position.
Macho, yet, oh so, fashionable.

Runs may be hard to get – but not admiring glances in this rakish ensemble

decked out in nice vivid pastel shades, y'know. Oz in green and yellow, you lot can be in red, white and blue if you like, the Windies in grey and maroon –'

'Excuse me, through the Chair, with respect, will not the West Indies have an unfair advantage in that one will be unable to see them in the dark?'

'Perhaps, there will be a system of traffic signals to tell you when their fast bowler is approaching. And he will be encouraged to smile a lot, and roll his eyes.'

'There'll be floodlights, you superannuated zombies. And the balls'll be white. Possibly luminous. So's you can see 'em whack the brightly-coloured helmets. And the blood'll show up.'

'Matron! Lord Parthenon if you please.'

'Blood and guts, mates, that's what the public wants. And action replays. Bloody great TV screens all round the ground with slow motion pictures from every bloody angle of helmets flying off, and batsmen doubling up and teeth being spat out. That'll get the crowds in, if the commercials don't. And *they'll* be pretty torrid. "Whack'em in the willies, Windies!" "Bomb the Poms! Plaster the Bastards!" and a lot of rock'n'roll and fast intercutting of the helmets and the teeth AND –'

'Matron! Matron! Colonel Roughage is foaming and frothing!'

'Through the Chair – Mr Pecker, where are you going to play these extraordinary fixtures? – your Controlling Body will not allow you on any decent cricket ground.'

'We don't need a decent bloody cricket ground – I've got a mobile wicket – a window-box on wheels. We can plant it any-where. Football grounds, car parks, botanical gardens – anywhere – AND – AND – I've had this bloody marvellous idea about the drinks interval. Who wants to see the twelfth man? We'll have a motorised trolley operated by topless girls with no brains at all.'

'Matron! Matron! For God's sake – salts and appliances!'

'AND – and you're going to love this. When a bloke is out for nought, apart from encouraging him to kick his stumps over and threaten the umpire with his bat, as he walks back to the Pavilion we get the camera up close to his face, so that we can see him wrestling with his emotions, and we superimpose a duck – an animated duck, pads, bat, little orange beak, it sheds a tear and follows him back and smoke comes out of its head. Isn't that great?'

'Matron! Oh, she's unconscious now.'

'People will come to love that little duck.'

'Through the Chair, will it be bleeding?'

'Aw, I like that. Thanks for the idea.'

'Mr Pecker, what you have described to us is not cricket, it is a circus. The Marylebone Cricket Club is not in the circus business. We are not Barnum and Bailey.'

'Through the Chair, they used to open the bowling for Essex. Bloody good.'

'What?'

'Stanley Barnum and Trevor Bailey. Bloody good.'

'Right, I'm off now. Going to audition ball-girls.'

'You won't get away with this, Pecker!'

'See you in court, fellas!'

MCC versus Tibet.

In 1921 the President of the MCC received this letter from Lt-Col. Ranulph Biggott, Treasurer of the British Himalayan Society.

Dear Sir,

Freddie Finistere-Strutt-Gore, with whom I think you were at Eton, has just returned from the Himalayas with what seems a very sporty notion and might prove to be right up your avenue. (He has also returned, we at the Society are proud to report, with a New World Record in that he is the first person to reach 25,000 feet or so on Mount Everest without oxygen or sherpas, and clad in only a silly woollen hat and tweeds – then again he was the first up Mrs Bradley without any of the aforementioned, so he was unlikely to experience either giddiness or apprehension.)

The very sporty notion – Freddie noticed during the expedition's rest-up in Tibet that the locals were very intrigued when the English mountaineers cobbled together a rude game of cricket. Some of them were invited to take part and showed a distinct talent for the Noble Game. Freddie immediately suggested to the Head Man there that the Tibetans might well enjoy playing host to the Marylebone Cricket Club. This idea tickled the fellow pink. He wondered what the reaction of the MCC might be. Madge fit? And the boys?

Yours sincerely,

Ranulph

Immediately, a Committee was set up to investigate the possibilities of sending a touring team to Tibet. Here are the minutes of that historic meeting.

Minutes of an Extraordinary Meeting of the MCC Committee.

'Item 17, Gentlemen. You've all read Biggott's letter, I imagine, this projected tour of Tibet.'

'Home, Mr Chairman, if I'm not wrong, of the prayer-wheel and the tango.'

'And the Whirling Dervish.'

'Through the Chair, I don't think the tango falls within the bailiwick of the Whirling Dervish.'

'The prayer-wheel is spot-on, though. Tibet is also, I fancy, home of the Lama.'

'Ghastly creatures, llamas. Spit in your eye, soon as look at you. Ask my wife.'

'Unlikely behaviour, surely, for Holy Men. Perhaps it's the altitude.'

'Peru? Bloody high. Thin air. Ball goes all over the shop.'

'Remember Mexico and the effect of the atmosphere on Henderson's Telling Lob?'

'Didn't come down for eight or nine minutes.'

The Effect of Altitude on Henderson's Telling Lob.

'Mexico had three different Presidents in the course of one over.'

'With respect, I don't think Peru comes into it. Or Mexico. Or the Whirling Dervish. Tibet is in the Himalayas somewhere. Perhaps someone would fetch the globe.'

'Righty ho. Round thing covered in red bits.'

'Mr Chairman, perhaps you could clear up the confusion on the lama front.'

'The spitting ones have two L's like Llanelly.'

'Llanelly 4 – Llamas 2.'

'Is that the final score? Bugger. I had them for a draw. Or was that the Casuals?'

'The question is should the MCC go to Tibet?'

'Of course, we should – we march t'wards where'er Leather meets King Willow. There are no boundaries –'

'We'll take our own. Make a note of that, Mr Secretary, for the Baggage-Master. Whitewash and a decent brush. Gentlemen, the Marylebone Cricket Club marches once more – to Tibet!'

(CHEERS and cries of 'What's yours, Gubby?')

The Old Billiard-Hall, Lhasa.

This is something religious thrown up hastily by the locals to ward off evil bouncers - and beamers.

This is myself - purveyor of such. The religious thing must have worked as I never hit one of the little Tibetan buggers.

My Tibetan Sketch Book.

Myself.

Umpire.
Klung.

P. E. Nodule.
(SURREY)

The Tibetan Opening Pair.

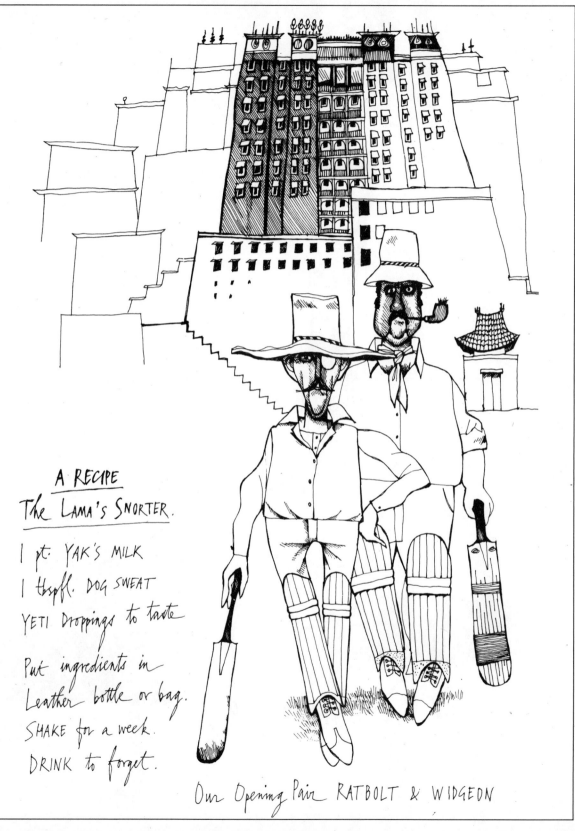

A RECIPE
The Lama's Snorter.

1 pt. YAK'S MILK
1 tbspfl. DOG SWEAT
YETI Droppings to taste

Put ingredients in
Leather bottle or bag.
SHAKE for a week.
DRINK to forget.

Our Opening Pair RATBOLT & WIDGEON

The Old Scoreboard and Tea-Rooms, Lhasa

The Old Scorer, Lhasa

The score, including sundries & Bowling Analyses are all IN HIS HEAD!

The Old Yak & Heavy Roller, Lhasa.

The Intolerably Long Run-up of Ransid Yakshpit.

MCC versus New Guinea.

Dear Lewis,

This is a tour you won't find evidence of in the archives. Far too messy. I've only been able to come up with odd gobbets. A letter to myself from the skipper, Digby Strutter-Stuffe, quite a useful all-rounder in his day, the letter to Mrs Peach, and a picture or two. I never heard another word from Digby, no more letters, and on his return he was almost immediately certified by his family and despatched to Coney Hatch, where he was not allowed visitors. The letter to Mrs Peach speaks volumes, and this photograph of Harry Charleston's autographed leg tells a very different story to Harry Charleston, who maintained to his death that he had no wooden legs, and that if he ever had lost a leg, which he had not, it would certainly not have been in Papua/New Guinea. Money passed hands in my view. See what you think.

Rambo Legge-Brake.

Dear Rambo,

By Heaven, what a long and tedious voyage from Darwin to Rabul. To make matters worse we were beset by a plague of flying-fish. It was asking for trouble to leave one's port-hole open. Fish-droppings in the tooth-mug are not the hall-mark of a luxury cruise in my book. Nor does fish-shit add anything to a tepid gin and tonic. But the privations we suffered on the grisly six-month voyage from Tilbury were as nothing compared to the horrors that awaited us in Papua.

Almost immediately upon arrival we were transported up-country in all manner of vehicles from an ancient charabanc to a pig-drawn trap. We were deposited by the side of the jungle road and abandoned to our fate. We were not alone, we could hear whispering and grunting and furtive movement emanating from the thick foliage. Not unnaturally we were filled with trepidation, we had read of some of the local practices, and we were some distance from civilisation.

We spent a very uncomfortable hour or so. Then there was a fearsome crashing as something approached us through the undergrowth. A quick straw-poll conducted amongst the team showed the majority opinion to be that it was some species of porker, though there was some doubt as to whether it was a wild boar or merely an irked domestic pig. It was neither, it was a tiny black man with fuzzy hair and a bone through his nose. Clearly, our host. Smiling broadly, he gestured that we should follow him into the jungle. After a steamy march of about a mile or so through thick bush, we came upon a small thatched wooden hut. If this was the Pavilion, there was no sign of the ground, just lowering greenery.

It *was* the Pavilion, and thick with pygmies, who seized our baggage and placed it in the hut. Once again our elfin host mimed that we should follow him. We did so, and it was not long before

we emerged into an oblong clearing, some twenty-five yards by five. It took some little time for it to dawn upon us that this was the pitch, a theory reinforced by the presence of crude stumps, one with a skull mounted on it.

I thought fielding was going to be the most hazardous aspect of the game. Not so. We tossed and I think we lost, though I am not familiar with the currency in those parts – the pig seemed to me to land on its back. However, we found ourselves in the field. When I say 'in the field', I mean – gathered on the pitch. I thought this the best idea – to pack the oblong and, should the ball be struck into the thick jungle, to send the fielders off in pairs or even threes to look for it. While I was setting my field, Charleston, a very useful medium-pacer from Kent, set off to mark out his run and that was the last we saw of him for three days.

We searched briefly, but felt we should press on with the game. It was then we were introduced to the bizarre Papuan sense of humour. Plover, who was to open the bowling from the other end, asked the umpire for the new ball. He was handed, with some ceremony, a round, rough, unpolished hairy object. 'What,' he asked of Prunehat and Gooseboot at mid-off, 'do they think this is?'

Gooseboot put his finger on it. '*I* think it's the shrunken head of Harry Charleston.'

Plover dropped it like a hot potato.

Prunehat swifly put the kibosh on this suggestion. Prunehat is much travelled. A decent shrunken head, he said, required some months of preparation and pickling. This could not be the last remains of Harry Charleston. The umpires were beside themselves with glee. Obviously, this is a well-worn local joke. We pretended to enjoy it.

'This is going to be a long tour,' I said to the lads in the dressing-room, 'among people with a very different sense of humour to ourselves. Smiling through, that must sum up our attitude. Smile through, chaps.'

How we laughed at the luncheon interval when Cook arrived at our table with what at first sight could so easily have been mistaken for a human leg.

Tomorrow we march further up-country.

Love,

Digby

This fellow was apparently quite the best batsman the MCC met on the tour of Papua/New Guinea. Does he remind you of anybody? Are you in a position to ask Vivian Richards if he has any Papuan relatives? Would you dare?

Telex: 297329 MCCG G
Telephone Nos.:

Pavilion	.. ..	01-289 1611-5
Indoor Cricket School		01-286 3649
M.C.C. Shop	.. ..	01-289 1757
Prospects of Play	..	01-286 8011
Tavern Caterers	..	01-286 2909
Tennis Court	.. ..	01-289 1288

Marylebone Cricket Club,

Lord's Ground,

London,

NW8 8QN

Dear Mrs Peach,

It is my unhappy lot as President of the Marylebone Cricket Club to inform you that while representing the Club in New Guinea, your husband Peach, L. B., was killed and, not to beat about the bush, eaten by natives. Until the rest of the team returns to this country, I am afraid that the facts surrounding the incident needs must be rather sketchy. Suffice it to say, he was a professional, and knew what to expect. It may somewhat soften the blow to report that he had scored a most solid 38 not out prior to lunch, and there is no doubt that had he survived that interval, he would have gone on to even better things in the afternoon session.

Needless to say, the Marylebone Cricket Club will be sending no more representative teams to New Guinea until there is firm evidence that they have changed their ways. Cannibalism, as such, is not on.

The whole Committee joins me in saying how sorry we are about poor Peach. I wonder if his name excited the gastric juices of the local team, we may never know.

Enclosed you will find a Postal Order for £3. A little something you will gather has been added to his salary for the tour, in spite of the fact that technically he did not complete it.

Yours sincerely,

Iris Bailey

pp. Sir Rambo Legge-Brake
(signed in his absence)

An Aerial View
of the Wicket.

A Full-Frontal
View of one of our
Opponents.

An Illuminating Incident in East Africa.

The MCC was touring East Africa, as I recall, suffice it to say we were up-country, many a mile from civilisation as we know it, staying at some hotel made entirely of wood, set beside a watering-hole. I was, for reasons I can no longer put a finger on, up a tree. It was night-time, drums were beating, beasts growling and barking, any of these may have been contributing factors. Anyway, I was suddenly aware that I was not alone. Below me I heard voices, detected, by the glow of two cheroots, they were members of our party enjoying a post-prandial. Not wishing to draw attention to the fact that I was up a tree, I did not halloo them, but remained mute. I'm glad that I did so, for I was thus able to enjoy their conversation, which I recorded on hotel note-paper upon my return. The conversation, to my mind, encapsulated the spirit of the Marylebone Cricket Club, and I am happy to report it to you verbatim. The protagonists were Charlie Vestibule (Cambridge University and Surrey) and Ralph Lather (Oxford and Kent) – a very useful opening pair. (They were in fact destined, within the week, to put on an opening stand of 793 against LXXXVII Assorted Black Fellows from wherever it was that we were.)

Lather: 'This is surely as good a time as any, Charlie, to ask what the advantages are, given the circumstances, thick jungle, restless natives, a million miles from Harrods, of being a member of the MCC?'

Vestibule: 'I'll tell you, Ralph. A blazer, and, to some extent, a cap which any indigenous native worth his salt would jump at.'

Lather: 'Do you mean, Charlie, "jump at" in the literal sense, teeth bared, eyebrows working, assegai at the ready, etc.? (Incidentally there goes another one. Rotten shot,

Sambo!) Or more the "Good Lord, Bwana-Johnny, for that cap I would give you my wives/camels/porkers whatever but not necessarily in that order"?'

Vestibule: 'The latter is the fellow, Ralph. They love red and yellow.'

Lather: 'You don't think the same effect could be created by being a Free Forester or decked out in I Zingari togs?'

Vestibule: 'Absolutely not! And you certainly don't get the same class of member.'

Lord PORKER adjusts his Field.

Lord Porker's Famous Over.

This over, the longest ever bowled, was bowled in the Final Test, a timeless Test, against Zanzibar in 1914. It was just before tea on the ninth day that Lord Porker decided to bowl an over himself. Zanzibar, put in to bat by Lord Porker, had batted for nine days and amassed some 270 runs for the loss of four wickets. Lord Porker's first ball was a dreadful long-hop and was struck for six. So angry was Lord Porker that the next twenty-seven balls were 'wides'. Further incensed, Lord Porker then began to throw the ball at the batsman, this resulting in 308 'no balls' before darkness fell. Day after day, this appalling display of petulance continued. The other members of the team pleaded that he retire hurt, or be certified a lunatic, as they wished to return to Old Blighty and lock horns with the Boche. Lord Porker then began to receive large numbers of white feathers, the suggestion being that he was only keeping the over going to avoid service at the front. The over finally ended in the winter of 1917 with Lord Porker's death.

Overs	Mdns	Runs	Wkts
0.1	0	7983	0

This pathetic aggregate is carved on a simple stone in the churchyard, in Cocks Balding, Hampshire.

Further Thoughts from Africa.

Incidentally, old cock, has it ever occurred to you, as it occurred to me suddenly and violently the other night while running the Philoshave over the Little Woman's back, that throwing in is what separates Man from the Gorilla? Gorillas can do many things, but throwing in slap over the stumps from forty yards or so – quite beyond them. Just thought I'd mention it.

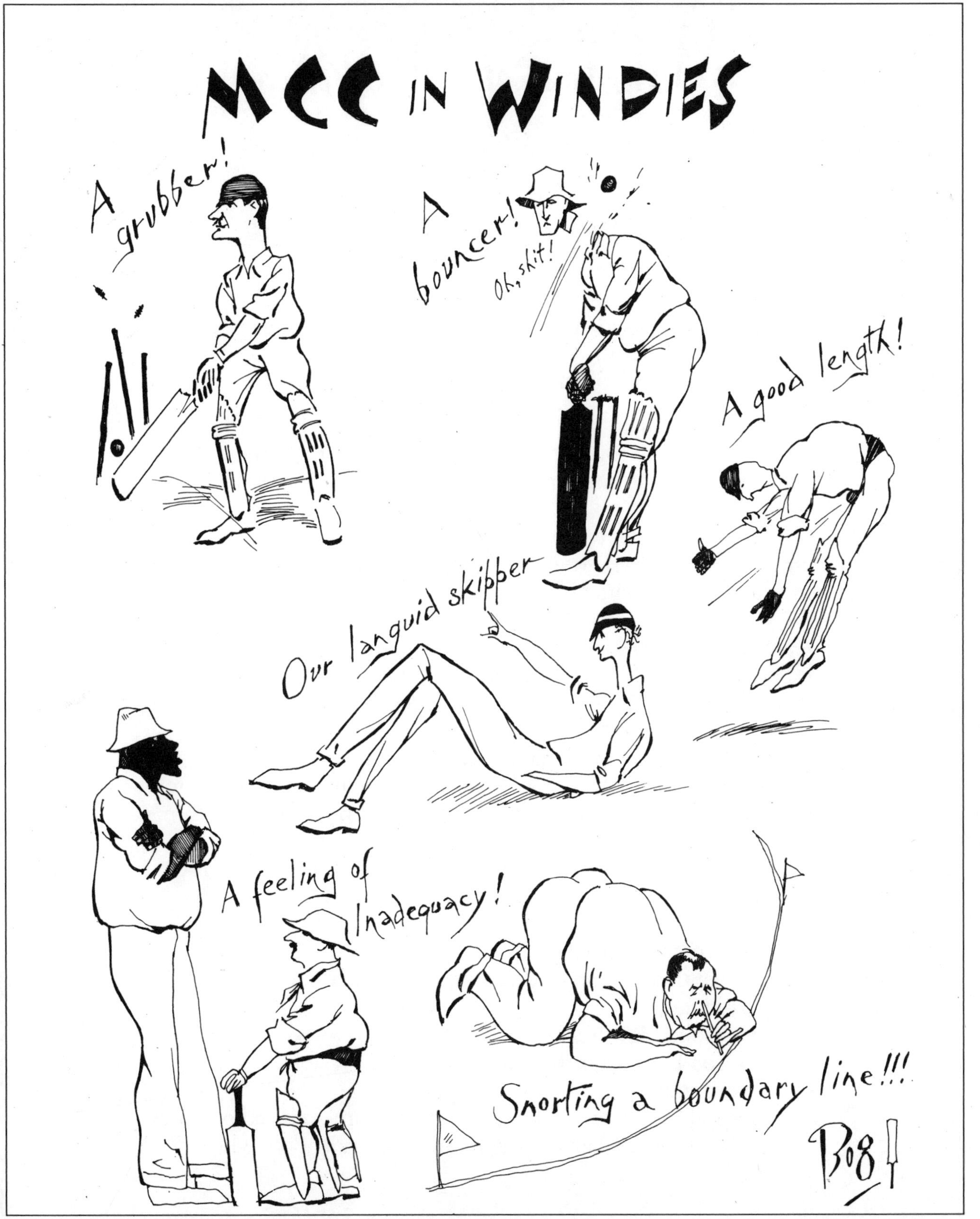
MCC IN WINDIES
A grubber!
A bouncer!
Oh, shit!
A good length!
Our languid skipper
A feeling of Inadequacy!
Snorting a boundary line!!!
Bog

Minutes of Meeting of Touring Committee.

In 1977, it was decided that the touring team would no longer be known as the MCC Touring Team, playing Test Matches as 'England', but henceforth be 'England' for all matches.

'Through the Chair, this is a grave and beastly step in the wrong direction. Apart from undermining the very grass roots of the game we love, it smacks, in my view, of Nationalisation, like British Rail.'

'It is a deliberate snook cocked at all those, alive and dead, who have journeyed to all corners of the globe, bag in hand, to raise aloft the colours of Marylebone.'

'It's also a damned silly idea, for whereas it's one thing for a team called Marylebone to lose to a New South Wales Country XI, it does very little for our National Pride when England, no less, are bustled out for 97 by a bunch of semi-literate, lager-soaked sheep-shaggers.'

'Point taken, Gentlemen, but I imagine that the feeling was that it is rather misleading for sixteen or seventeen players to tour about as the Marylebone Cricket Club when none of them comes from Marylebone.'

'Fewer and fewer, Mr Chairman, come from *England*, God knows.'

'Harsh words!'

'But true! But true!'

'I trust this is in no way an attack upon that fine Scot, Sir Alec Douglas-Home?'

'Or Colin Cowdrey, who is Indian.'

'Is Ted Dexter not Uruguayan?'

'Near enough.'

'I speak of all those South Africans, Zambians, Rhodesians, Barbadians, Trinidadians, Uruguayans and Icelanders who are as yet unborn but will doubtless one day sport the three lions of England.'

'What has all this to do, through the Chair, with the price of fish?'

'Turks and Lithuanians, Comanches and Sioux, Welshmen –'

'Pardon my interrupting your catalogue of the various colours, classes and creeds that may soon be eligible to play Test cricket for England, but is this not a very sound argument for our handing over the reins? I hardly see Lithuanians or what-you-will getting past our Membership Committee. It's hard enough for Welshmen.'

'Here! Here! (or is it "Hear! Hear!") The Marylebone Cricket Club certainly draws the line at foreigners.'

'Well, in fairness, we do make exceptions. Duke of Edinburgh, that sort of thing.'

'Some of them polish up quite decently.'

The Museum at Lord's.

Curator Testice is our Knowledgeable Guide.

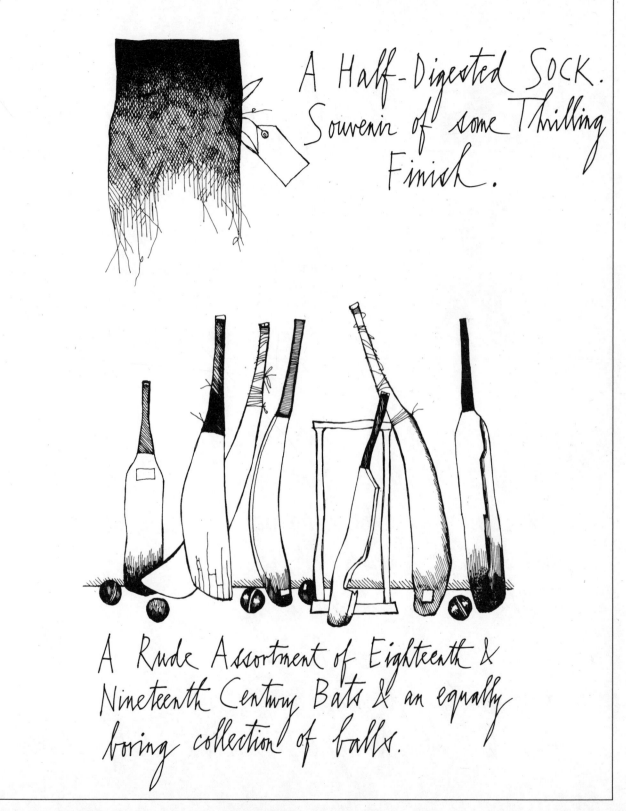

A Half-Digested SOCK.
Souvenir of some Thrilling
Finish.

A Rude Assortment of Eighteenth &
Nineteenth Century Bats & an equally
boring collection of balls.

The UNCENSORED Ashes

The ASHES

We Stuffed the Pommy Bastards
We Screwed their Pommy
[brains
We Barbecued the Doctor's
[Box
& Here's the bloody remains

These are the ASHES as originally presented to M.C.C. by some offensive Australian women. Whether or not it contains what it advertises or a number of Abos or burnt bails is immaterial and who wants to look?

NOT as you might think the UMBRELLA HANDLE that was bitten through by a MEMBER during the famous Ashes Test, but one broken in the LONG ROOM by Sir Rambo, demonstrating to DAVID GOWER How to Waft Airily outside the Off Stump.

Mike BREARLEY'S BRAIN

The Ballet Rambo.

Choreography by
Sir Frederick Trueman

Music by a number of Swedes

Play Up!

A Ballet in Five Days

Based on a POEM by Sir Henry Newbolt

"The Old Red & Yellow"
A Ditty.

When I throw a plate of custard at a military band,
When I see a red-faced colonel lying prostrate in the sand,
What do I see? Red and Yellow.
What does it mean to me?
It means Marry-Maryleboney – It means the MCC.

When I see a London bus run o'er an elderly Chinee,
Or I see a telephone booth full of last year's kedgeree,
What do I see? etc.

When the quarantine flag rises 'gainst a red sky in the East,
When a matador lies bleeding, sand-blasted by the beast,
What do I see? etc.

When jaundice strikes and one's prescribed a course of
    scarlet pills,
When someone's pouring ketchup o'er a field of daffodils,
What do I see? etc.

When I see canaries flutter on Moscow's chilly breeze,
Or an avid toper's nose pressed into festering Froggy cheese,
What do I see? etc.

When I see pus emanating from a vicious-looking boil,
Or a ripe tomato floating in a sea of castor oil,
What do I see? etc.

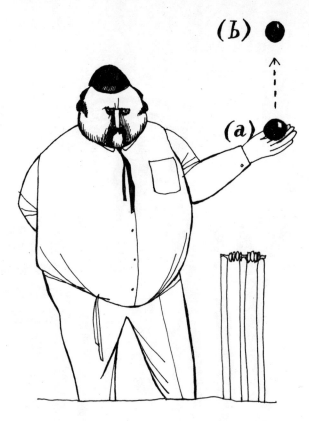

'INTIMIDATION'
Ashley Beamer (Gloucs & England)
sizes up his target.

An illustration from Sir Rambo
Legge-Brake's Instructional Manual
"Playing the Marylebone Way"

(M.C.C. Prods – £25.18.6d)